¿Me dejas tener una mascota?

por Gwendolyn Hudson Hooks • ilustrado por Lisa Cinelli

traducido por Esther Sarfatti

Bebop Books

An imprint of LEE & LOW BOOKS Inc.

¿Me dejas tener una mascota?

¿Me dejas tener un mono?

¿Me dejas tener un tigre?

¿Me dejas tener una cebra?

¿Me dejas tener un oso?

¿Me dejas tener un león?

¿Me dejas tener un pez? ¡Sí!

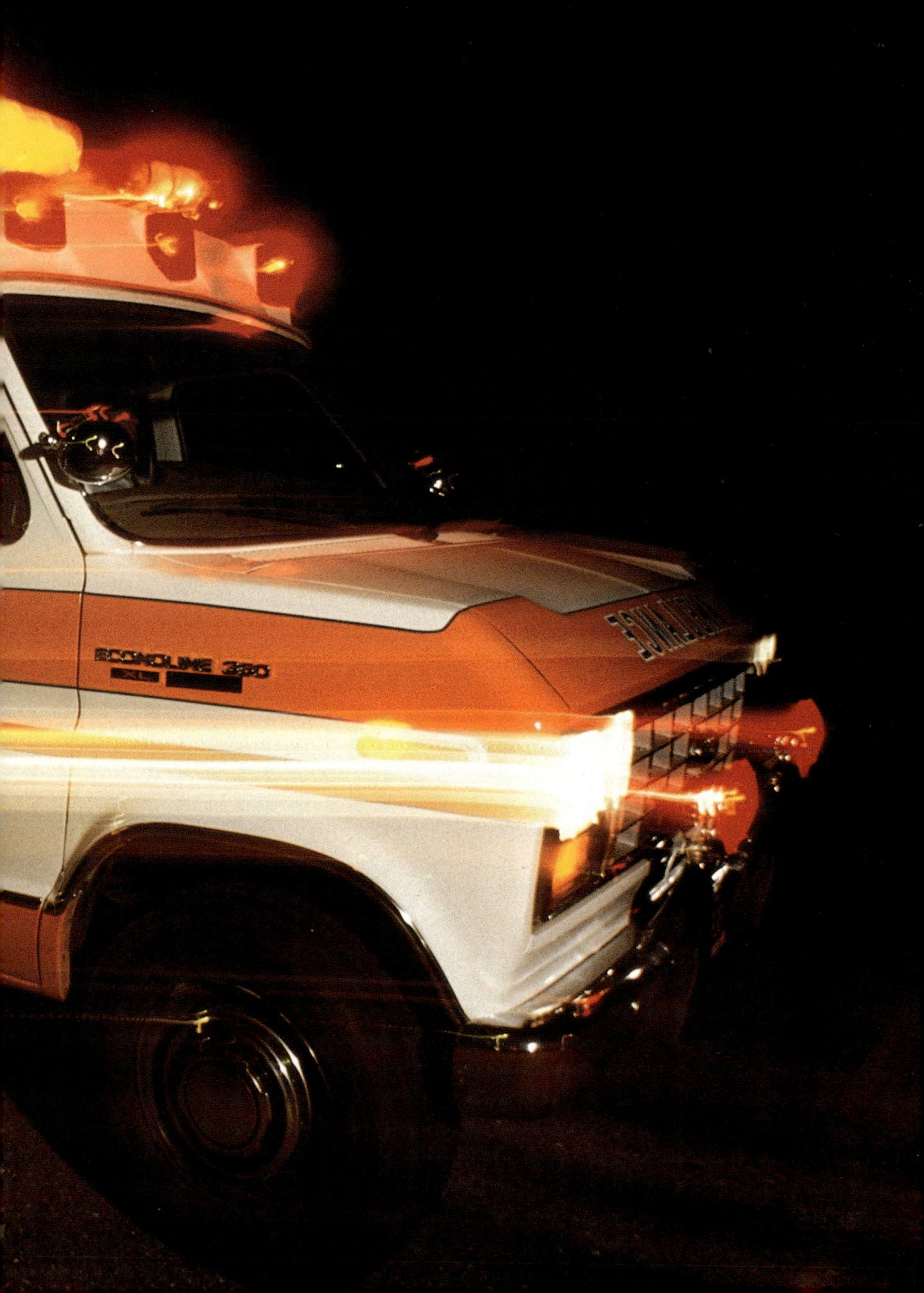

Franklin Watts Inc
387 Park Avenue South
New York, NY 10016

Library of Congress Cataloguing-in-Publication Data
Barrett, Norman S.
    The picture world of ambulances / Norman Barrett.
        p.   cm. — (Picture world)
    Summary: Describes ambulances and how they are equipped to treat
the sick and injured.
    ISBN 0–531–14090–3
    1. Ambulances—Juvenile literature.   [1. Ambulances.]   I. Title.
II. Series.
TL235.8.B37   1991
616.02'5—dc20   90–31223
                                                                          CIP AC

Designed by
K and Co.

Photographs by
International Red Cross
City of New York Emergency
    Medical Service
Australia House
Central Australian Aviation
    Museum
Atlas Conversions
N.S. Barrett Collection
Bell Helicopter Textron
Express Newspapers
Ford
MBB
Metropolitan Police
New York City Police Department
Westland
Split Second
Syndication International
ZEFA Picture Agency

Technical Consultant
Charles Keevil

The Picture World of

Ambulances

Norman Barrett

CONTENTS

Introduction	6
Emergency ambulances	8
Special ambulances	14
Major incidents	16
Air ambulances	18
Ambulances at war	22
Ambulances on the spot	24
Transport ambulances	25
Facts	26
Glossary	28
Index	29

Franklin Watts

New York • London • Sydney • Toronto

Introduction

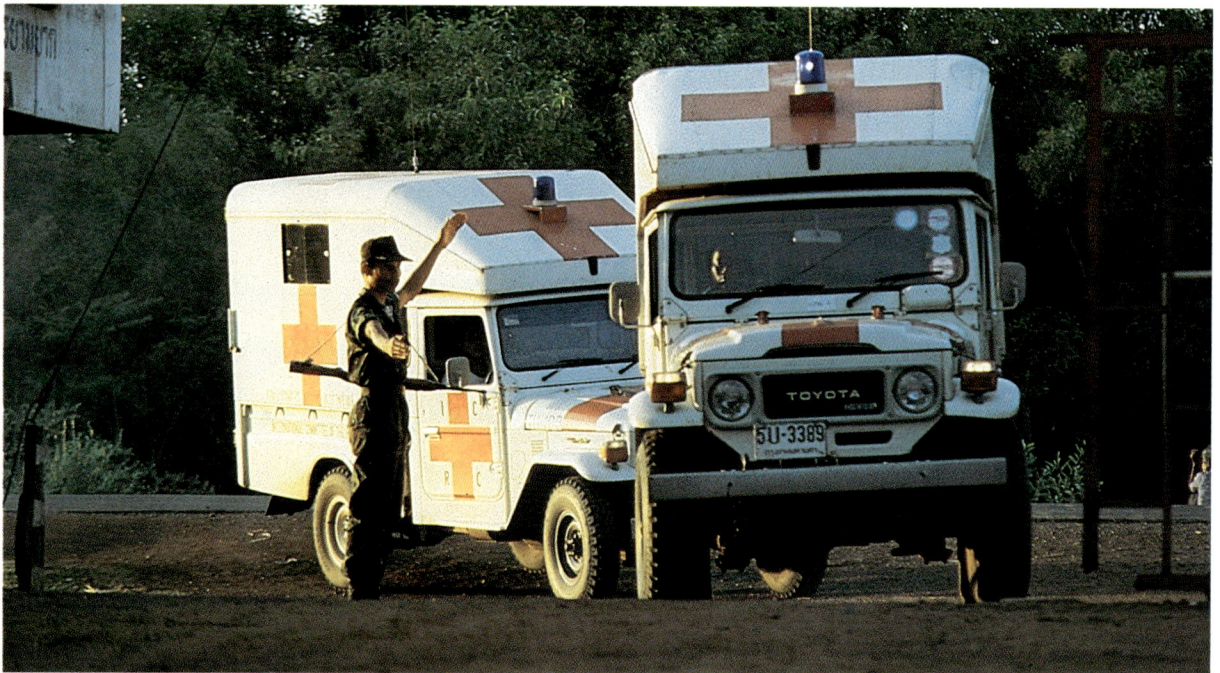

Ambulances are vehicles used mainly for taking sick or injured people to the hospital. Modern ambulances carry emergency medical equipment for treating patients on the spot and on the way to the hospital. Highly trained ambulance crews, called paramedics, give emergency treatment.

Specially equipped helicopters and planes also serve as ambulances.

△ Red Cross ambulances arrive at a checkpoint in northern Thailand. The Red Cross, an international organization, provides medical help around the world, wherever it is needed.

▷ Inside a typical emergency ambulance. There are two stretchers that serve as temporary beds while the patients are being taken to the hospital. First aid equipment includes lifesaving equipment, dressings, splints, and medicines.

▽ A helicopter on the scene of a farming accident. Helicopters can fly to and from remote places quickly.

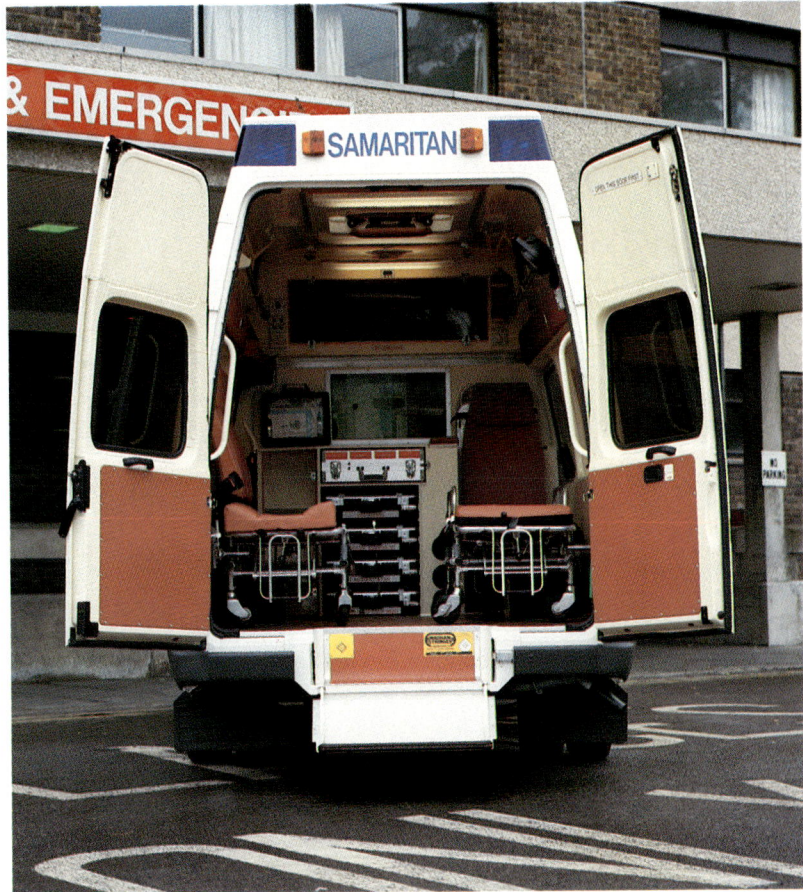

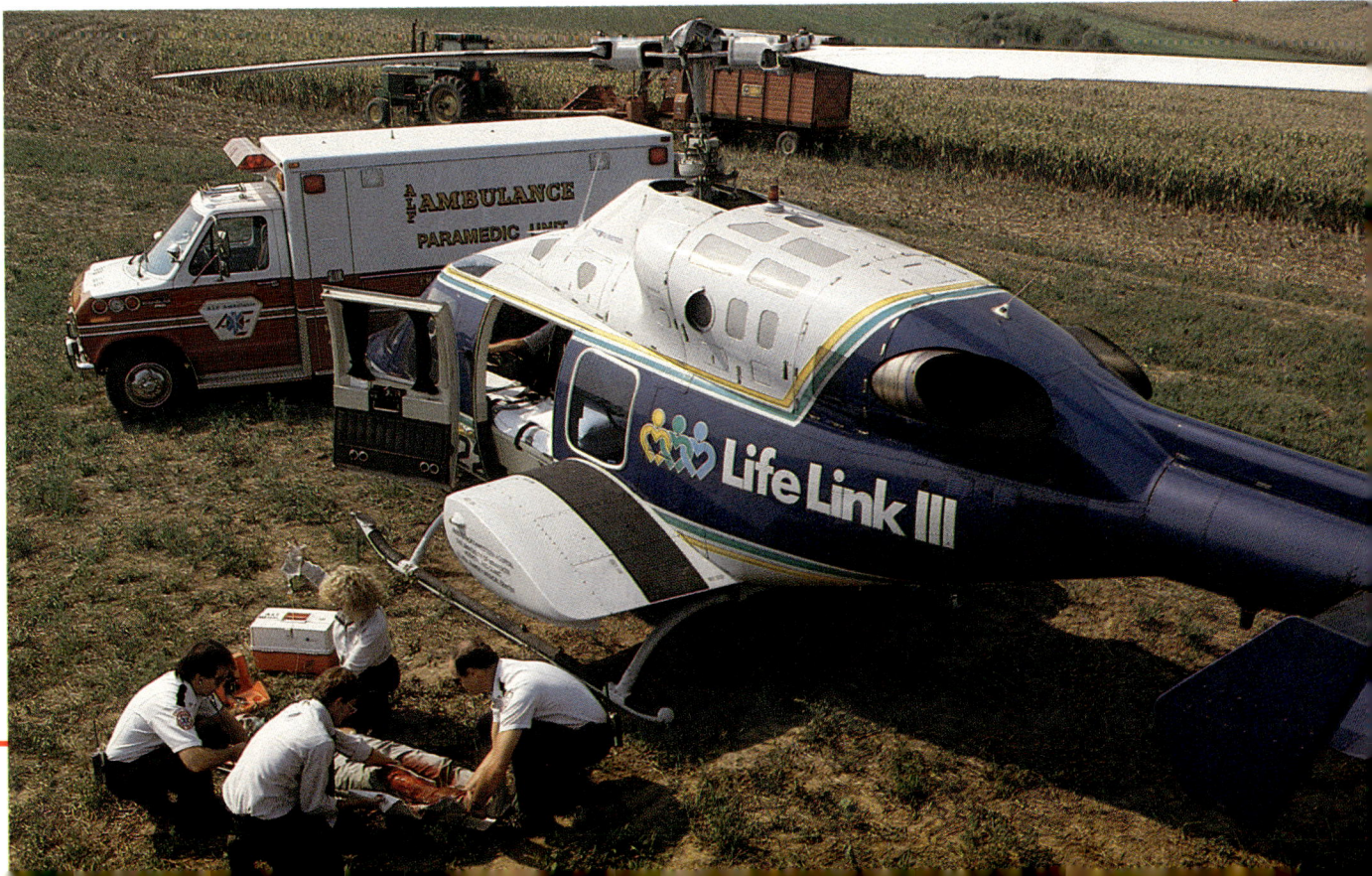

Emergency ambulances

Emergency ambulances go quickly to where they are needed. They respond to private calls when someone becomes ill in a public place or is injured. Or they may be required to speed to the scene of a major accident or other disaster.

Ambulances have their own communications center, which handles emergency calls over a wide area. Staff are also in contact with police and fire departments.

▽ Police and ambulance crews work together at the scene of a mock-up accident. The two agencies and the fire department co-operate closely during real incidents.

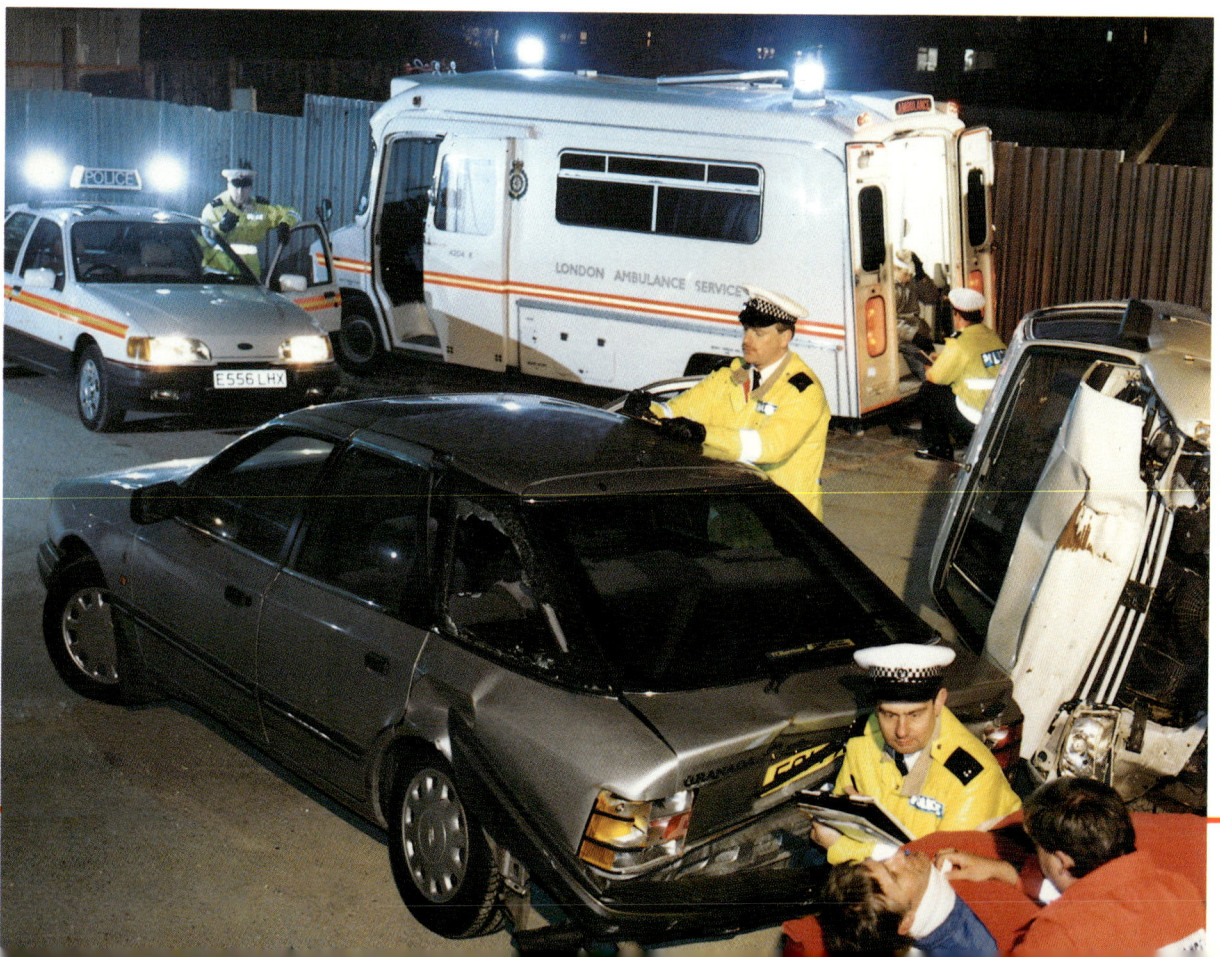

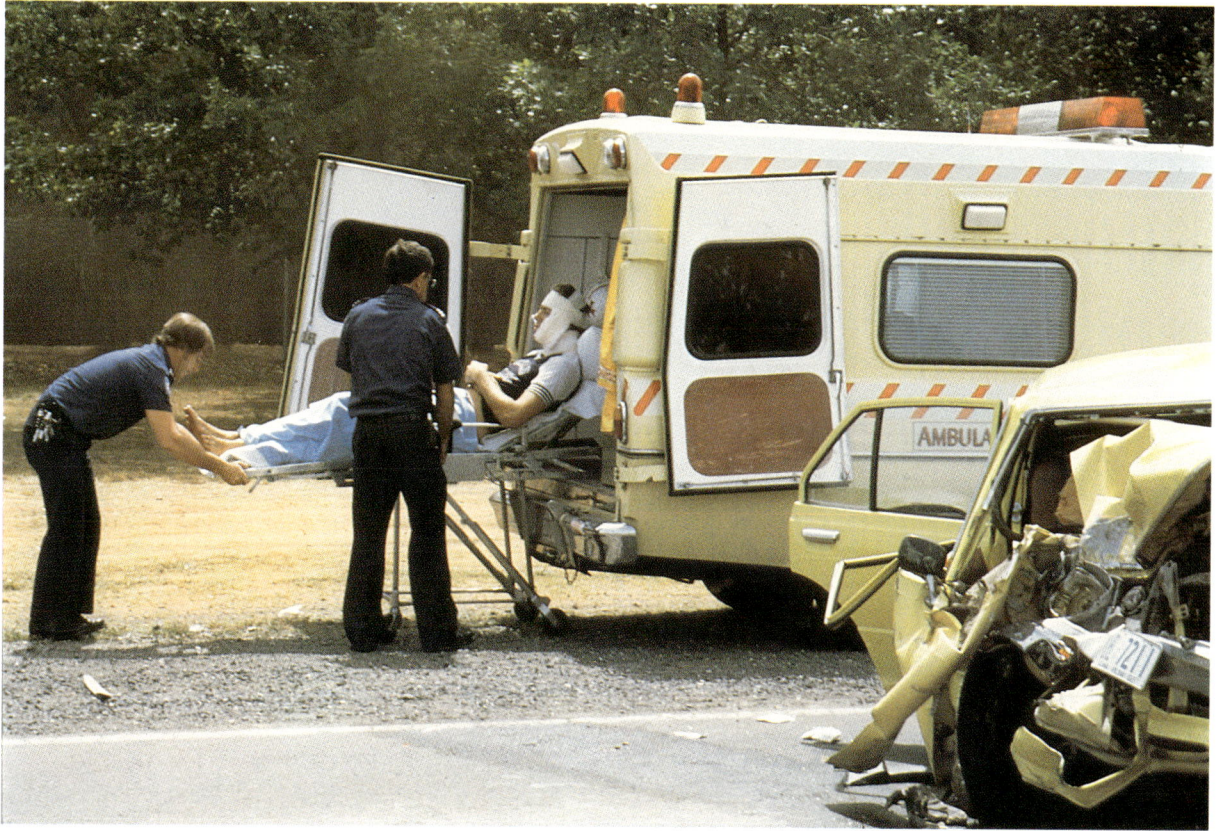

Paramedics give medical treatment to prepare a patient for moving. The equipment they use includes a resuscitator (breathing machine), defibrillator (heart machine), and aspirator (suction unit for clearing out the throat). They continue to treat the patient on the way to the hospital.

Paramedics may also contact hospital staff, preparing them for the case and perhaps taking advice from hospital doctors.

△ A victim of a road accident is carefully wheeled into an ambulance after being made as comfortable as possible.

9

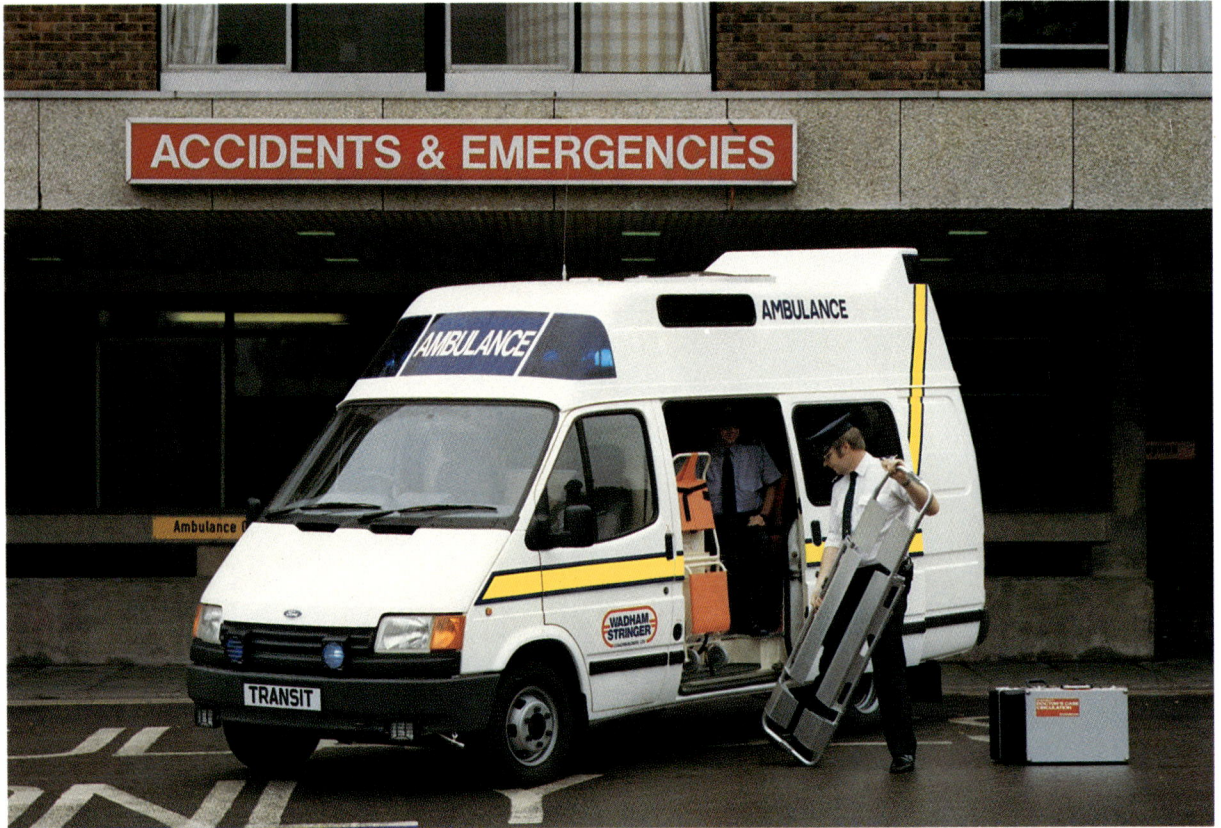

Most ambulances are purpose-built vans or trucks. They are painted with signs and equipped with flashing lights, sirens, and horns to warn other motorists to let them pass.

Modern ambulances have two-way radios so that they are in contact with their dispatchers.

Special helicopters are being used more and more for emergency ambulance work.

△ An ambulance based on a Ford Transit chassis, with special bodywork built by another company, Wadham Stringer. The yellow strips are made of material that glows in the dark.

△ Helicopter ambulances operate over areas impossible to reach by road.

▷ A helicopter ambulance with its rear clamshell doors open, showing the amount of medical equipment that can be carried.

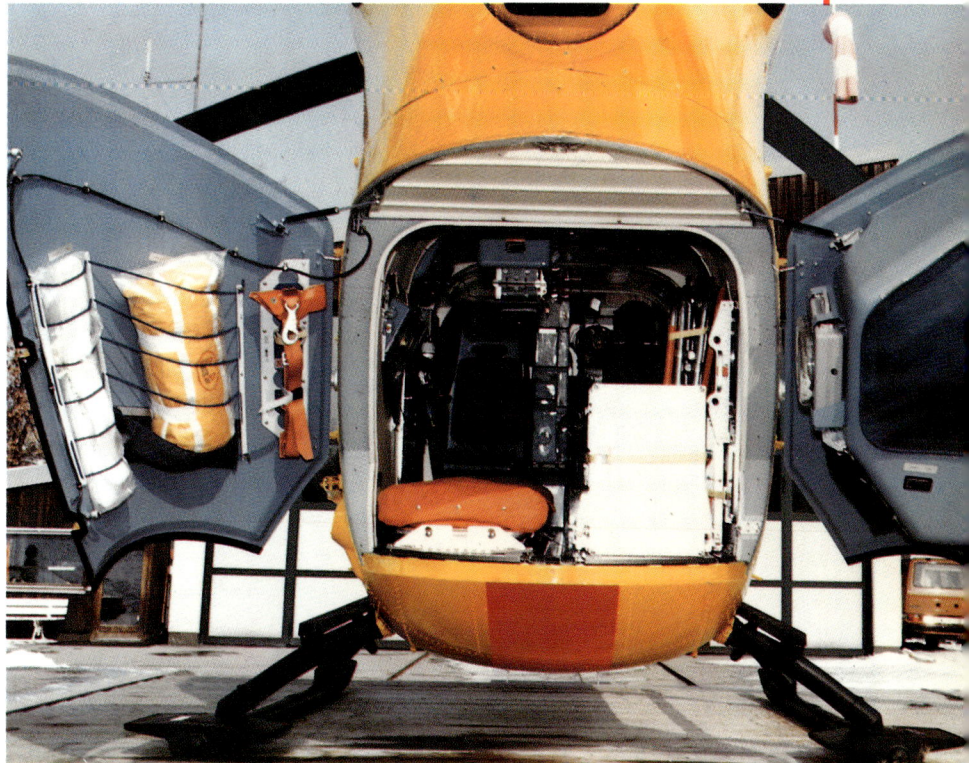

◁ Inside the cab of an emergency ambulance, the driver is in touch with central control.

▷ Inside, the ambulance is equipped with everything that might be needed in an emergency, including life-saving drugs and machines to keep patients breathing or regulate their heartbeats.

◁ In some areas, both the driver and the attendant are fully trained paramedics.

Lockers on the outside of the ambulance are used for stowage of equipment, such as an oxygen cylinder (above) and a stretcher (right).

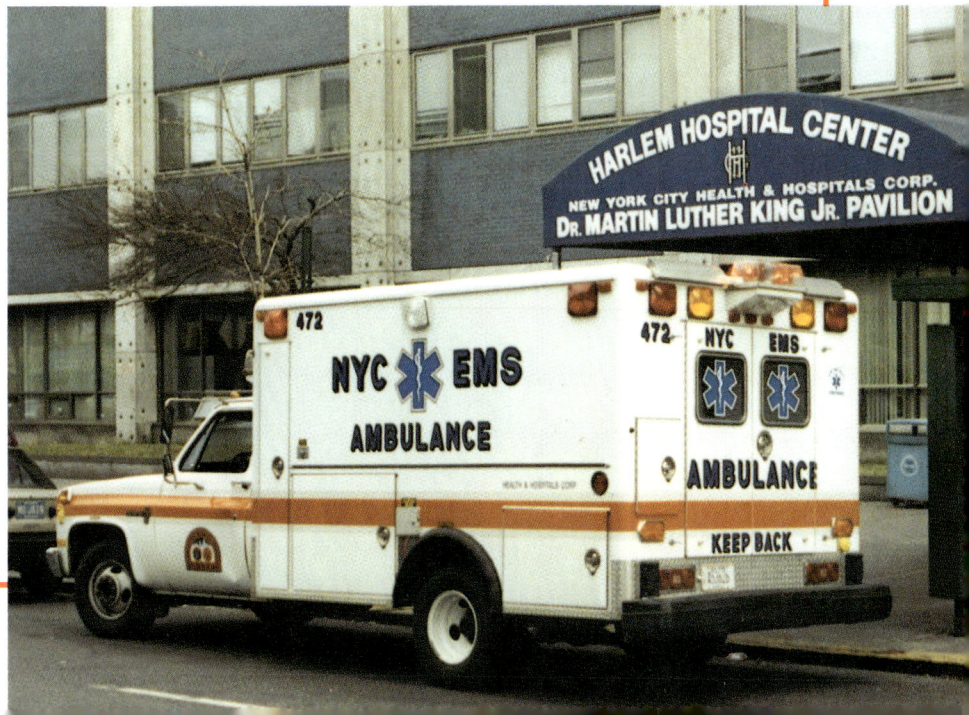

▷ The modern emergency ambulance is like an operating theatre on wheels. Instead of side windows, there is storage space both inside and out.

Special ambulances

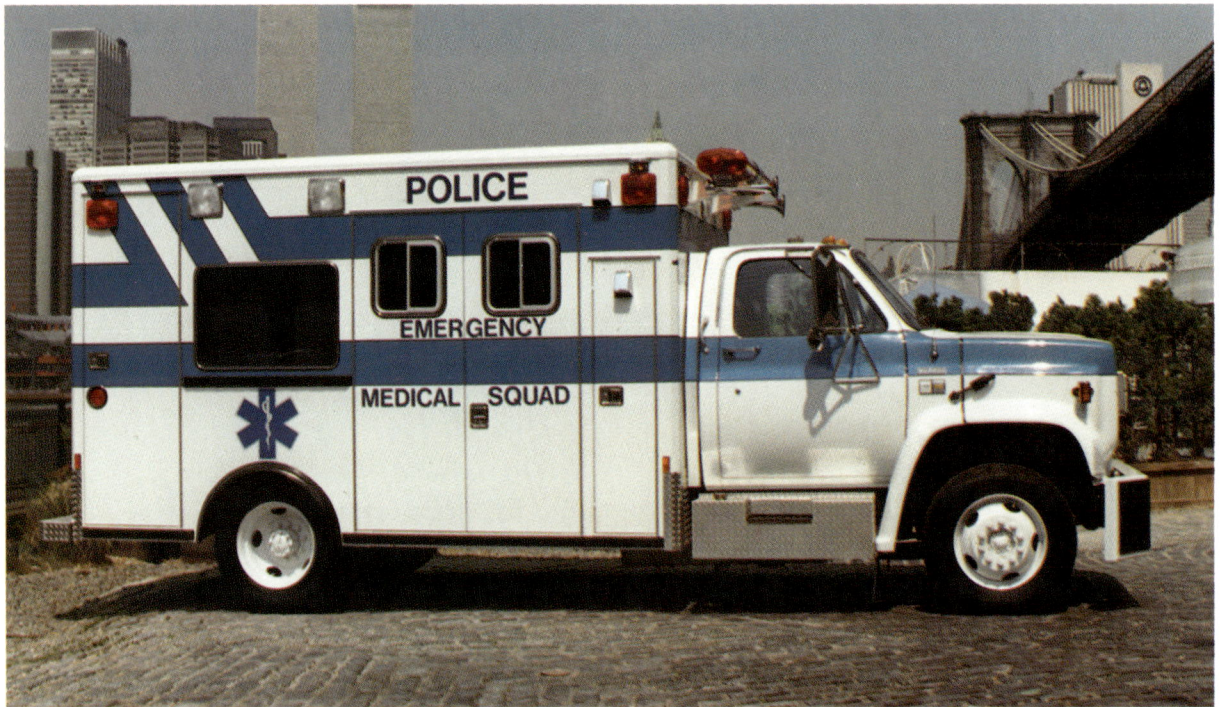

Some ambulances are built for special purposes, such as for use over rough country or in mountain rescue. Some are converted estate cars, used for taking a single patient on a long journey or at high speed between hospitals.

Special ambulances are used by some police forces. Organizations such as the Red Cross and the St John Ambulance Brigade also have their own ambulances.

△ An ambulance of the New York Police Department. Some police forces have their own medical squad to treat injured police personnel and take them to hospital.

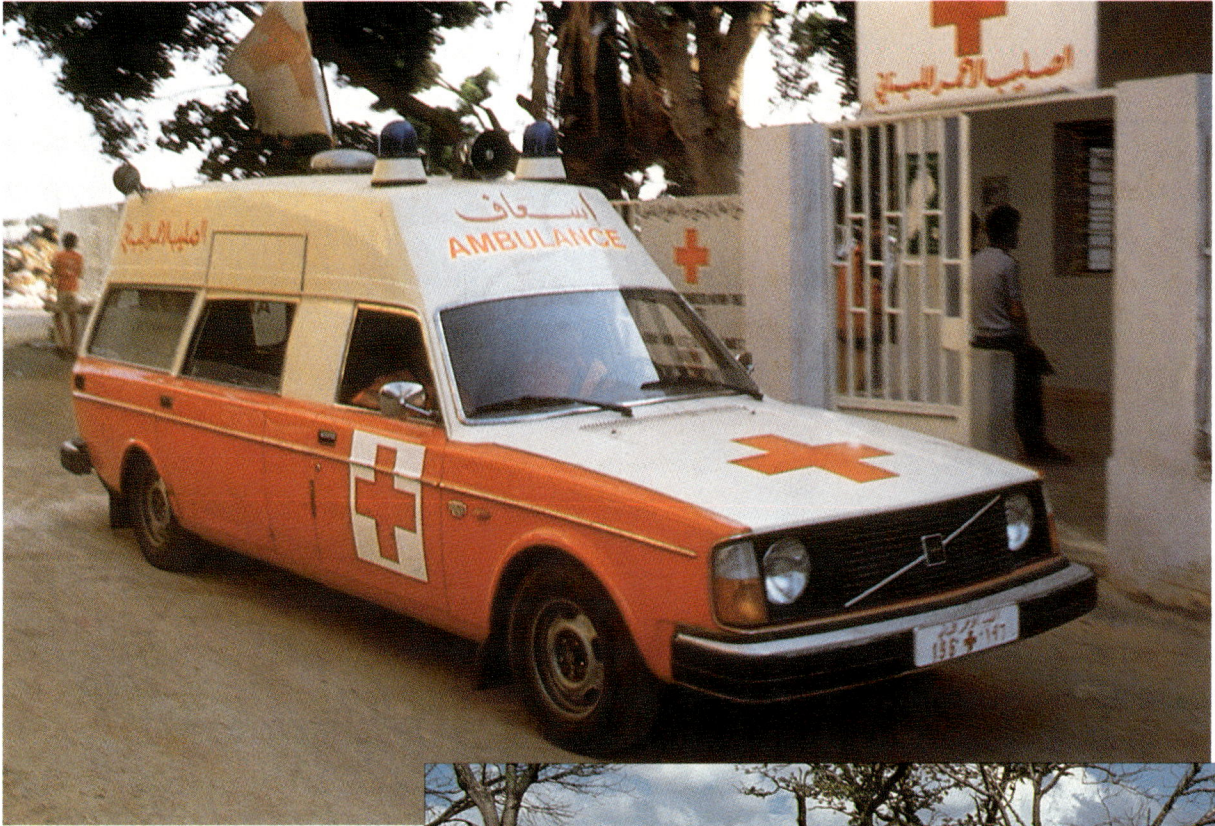

△ An ambulance of the Red Cross, a converted version of a Volvo estate car.

▷ A van used by the Red Cross as a baby care clinic in Botswana, in southern Africa.

Major incidents

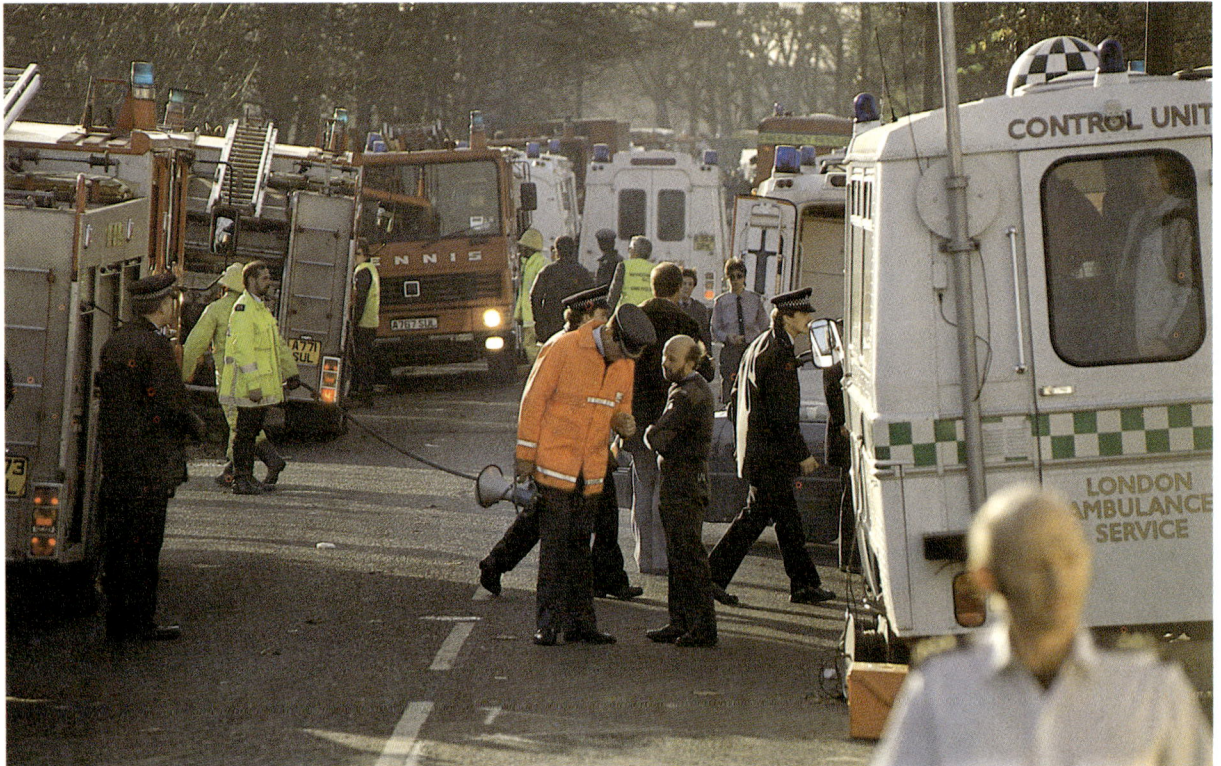

At a major accident with many casualties, a mobile communications center may be set up. This unit coordinates all the ambulance activity and keeps in contact with the other emergency services — police and fire. It also serves as a base for medical teams.

All nonurgent ambulance work in the area is delayed, and extra equipment is brought to the scene.

△ A mobile ambulance communications center (right) at the scene of a major train crash. This serves as the medical headquarters. It controls all the ambulances and links up with the fire and police departments.

All areas have special plans for major emergencies, such as train or plane crashes, or natural disasters such as floods or earthquakes.

Extra emergency equipment is brought to the scene in special vehicles. Emergency packs containing everything from hacksaws to hot water bottles are taken. The usual medical equipment is carried, but with extra blood, oxygen, drugs for pain relief, and splints and dressings of all kinds.

▽ Nurses and paramedics attend to survivors of a major train accident as the victims arrive at a hospital. Blood and oxygen continue to be given to a patient.

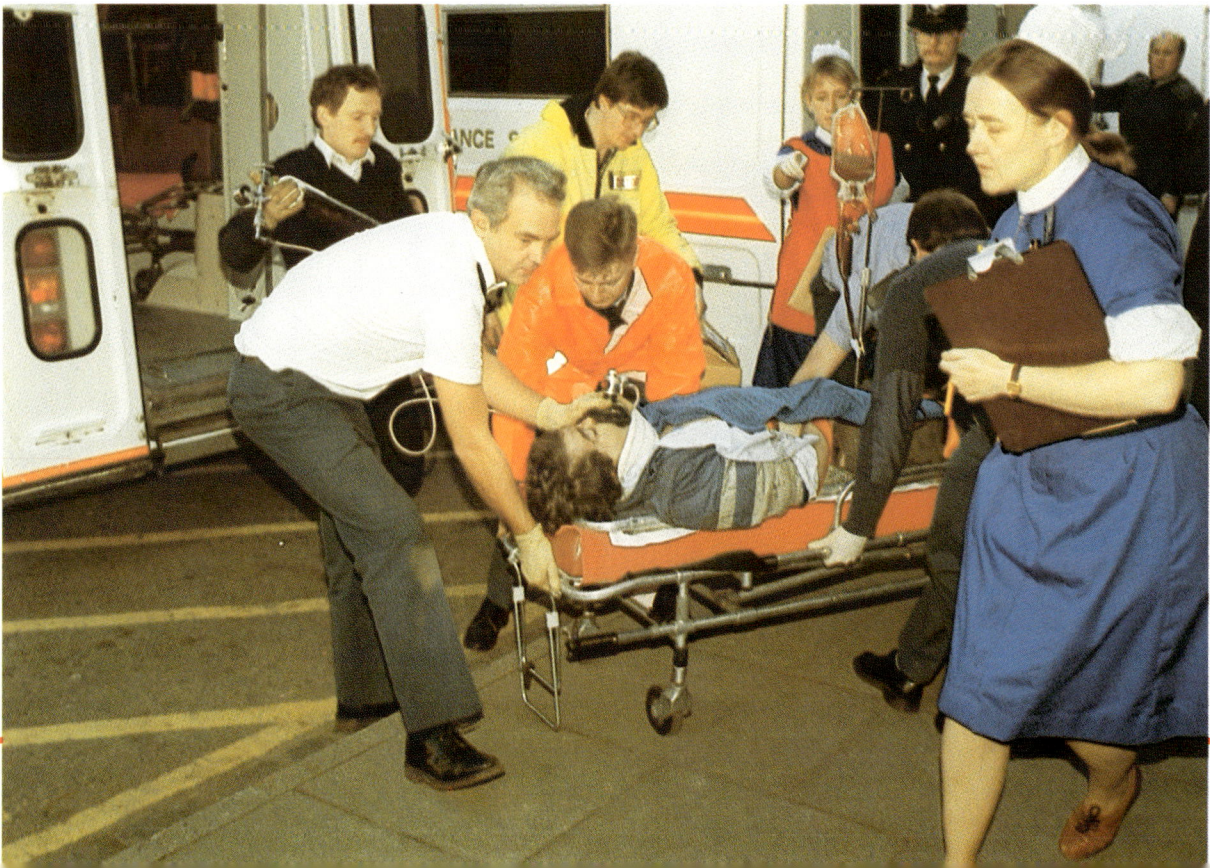

17

Air ambulances

Airplane ambulances can travel long distances quickly and are used for reaching cases in remote areas. Helicopter ambulances are used for carrying patients across the sea, or over rough or mountainous country. They can reach difficult places and land almost anywhere.

They are crewed by paramedics and are fully equipped to handle all medical emergencies. Like road ambulances, they keep in contact with medical staff at the hospital.

▷ A patient is wheeled into a helicopter ambulance with paramedics in attendance.

▽ The inside of a flying ambulance has been described as a "mini-emergency room in the sky."

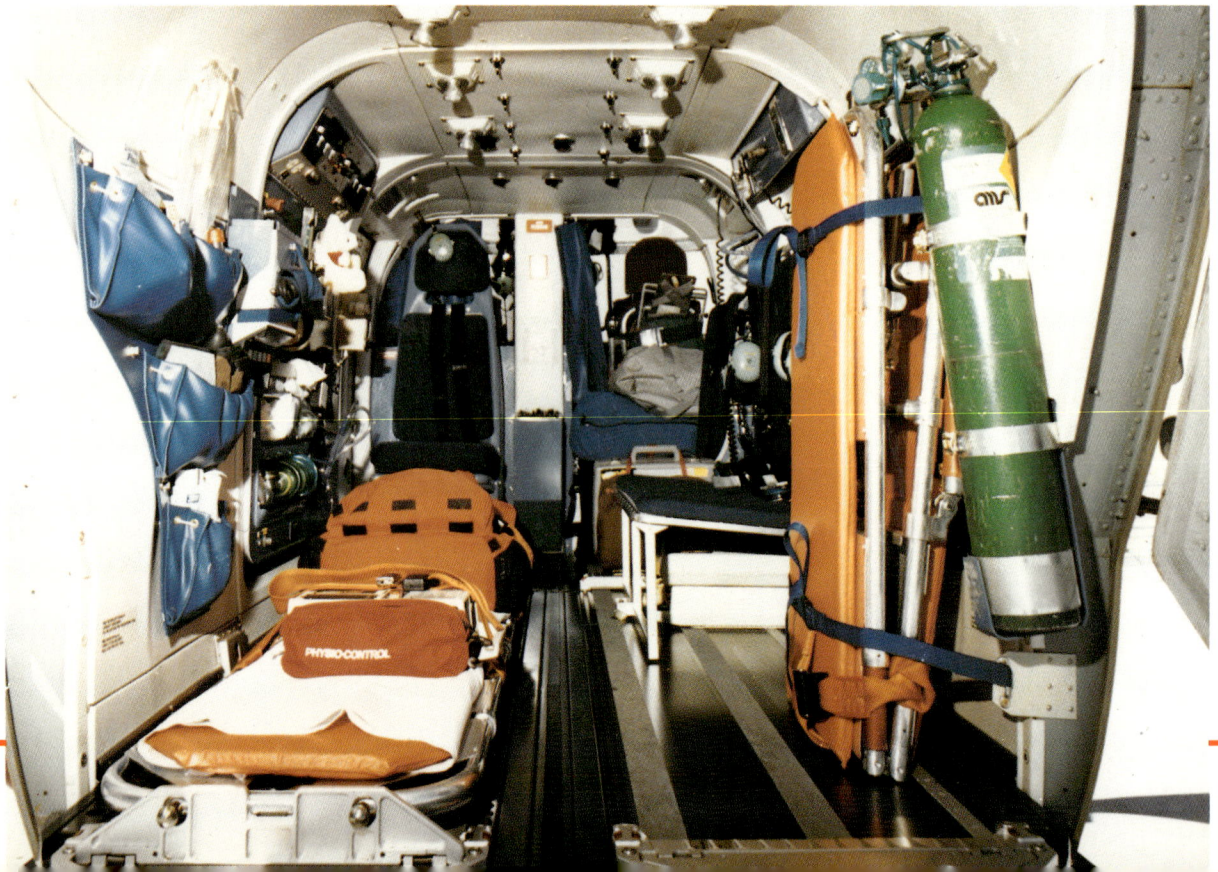

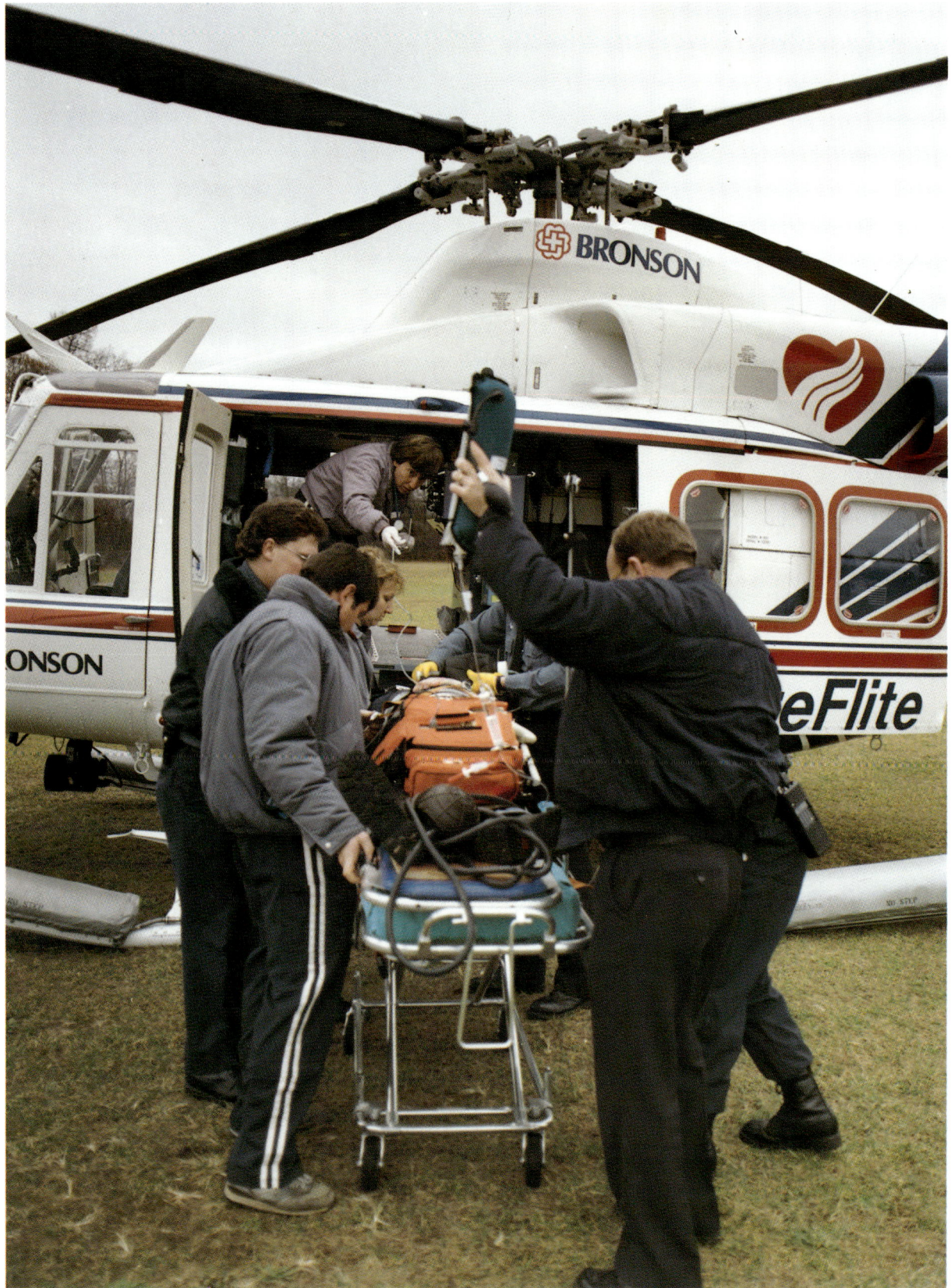

◁ Helicopter ambulances may be used to take crash victims to the hospital when roads are blocked with traffic.

Ambulances at war

Wherever fighting takes place, ambulances are needed to move injured troops or civilians away from the battlefield.

Specially equipped ambulances and helicopters are used to take the injured from the "front line" to hospitals and first aid stations away from the fighting.

The Red Cross Society sends its ambulances and medical staff to all parts of the world where they are needed in time of war.

▽ An army ambulance looks out of place on city streets, but they are sometimes used for civilian purposes in emergencies. Military ambulances have to be built like armoured cars for battlefield action.

△ Helicopter ambulances are used for evacuating injured soldiers from the battlefield.

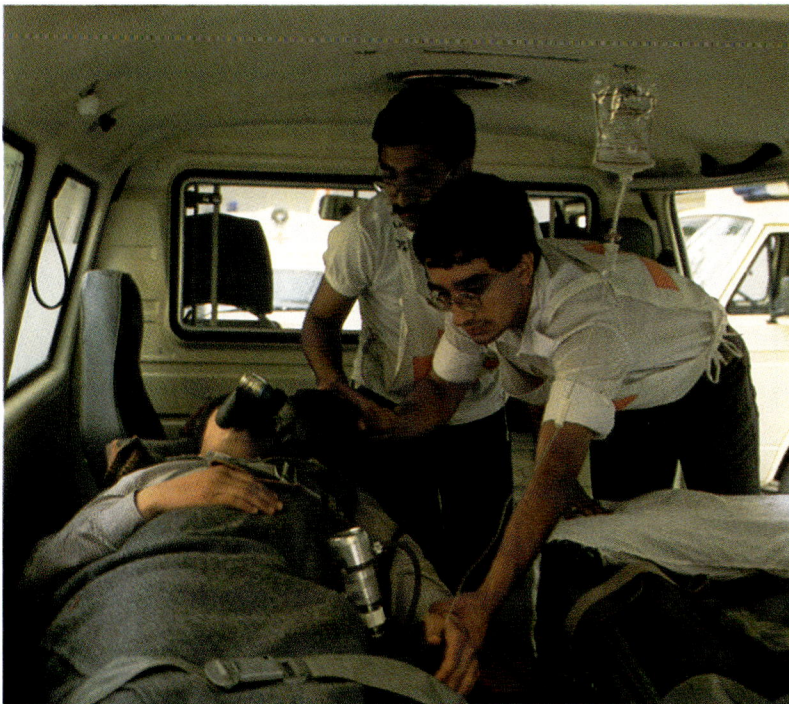

◁ A victim of the fighting in Lebanon is treated inside a Red Cross ambulance.

Ambulances on the spot

At big events, where large crowds of people are involved, ambulances wait on standby in case they are needed.

First aid stations at major sporting events, ceremonies or rock concerts deal with minor injuries or illness. But ambulances are always needed in the event of more serious cases to take the patients to the hospital.

In some countries, this standby ambulance service is provided by voluntary organizations.

▽ Ambulances on standby at a soccer game. The St. John Ambulance Brigade is a voluntary service providing first aid and emergency ambulances at public events. A British organization, it has spread to other parts of the world.

Transport ambulances

Ambulances are not used just for emergencies. An important task of ambulance services is the transportation of patients.

Patients who find it difficult or impossible to get around by themselves are taken to hospital appointments or day centers for the elderly or handicapped. Many transport ambulances (ambulettes) carry passengers in wheelchairs.

△ A small ambulance – converted from a van or station wagon – is used for transporting people in wheelchairs. The ramp at the back is raised electrically. Ambulances used for transportation work are called ambulettes. Their drivers are not as highly trained as emergency crews.

Facts

The Flying Doctor

Ambulance aircraft are operated by Australia's Royal Flying Doctor Service. They provide an emergency medical service for people living in remote areas – about two-thirds of the continent.

The service has 14 bases across Australia, and is a vital lifeline to more than 100,000 people each year. Without it, many Australians would be faced with a round trip of up to 1,000 km (600 miles) to their nearest doctor.

△ A Flying Doctor aircraft at the Central Australian Aviation Museum. The service has been in operation since 1928.

Fever ambulances

In the last century, people seriously ill with infectious diseases were taken to hospital in regular horsedrawn cabs. This put other people using the cabs at great risk of infection. It was not until the 1860s that special carriages were designed for the purpose. These fever ambulances were painted inside and had rubber pillows and mattresses so that the whole vehicle could be thoroughly scrubbed and disinfected after each patient.

△ A carriage designed in 1867 for taking fever patients to hospital.

The first ambulances

The first special carriages for the sick were horsedrawn wagons used for transporting injured soldiers in Spain about 500 years ago.

Steam ambulances were first built in 1902, but motorized ambulances began replacing the horsedrawn carriages in 1904.

△ A motorized police ambulance in London in the early 1900s.

The Red Cross
In 1859, a Swiss traveller, Jean Henri Dunant, was horrified to see the suffering of the wounded after a battle in Italy. He formed a group of volunteers to help them, and from this small beginning founded the international Red Cross five years later.

With its headquarters in Geneva, Switzerland, the movement now has societies in more than 130 countries. It provides medical help, equipment and ambulances in all parts of the world, in both peace and war.

△ A fleet of ambulances of the Cuban Red Cross stand in front of a specially equipped Red Cross plane.

Ambulance in space
A special "ambulance spaceship" may soon be needed. When several astronauts begin to stay in space stations for months at a time, the chances of becoming ill are much greater than with short space flights. The idea of a space ambulance, capable of bringing back astronauts in a matter of hours, is being discussed by scientists planning the new international *Freedom* space station for the late 1990s.

Glossary

Air ambulance
A special helicopter or plane outfitted with the emergency equipment, drugs, and dressings necessary to treat patients and keep them alive on the way to the hospital. Air ambulances are crewed by paramedics.

Ambulette
An ambulance used for transport work.

Aspirator
A suction pump used for clearing a patient's throat to restore breathing.

Defibrillator
A machine that applies an electric shock to the chest or heart to restore a patient's regular heart pattern.

Mobile communications center
A vehicle used at major incidents to coordinate all ambulance work and medical services and link up with other emergency services.

Oxygen cylinder
Oxygen cylinders provide a supply of oxygen for patients who are having trouble breathing. They are used with a resuscitator, which regulates the supply.

Paramedics
Trained ambulance crew qualified to give more than just basic first aid. Paramedics can administer drugs, give injections, and use specialized equipment to keep patients breathing or to regulate their heartbeats.

Resuscitator
Apparatus used to restore and regulate a patient's breathing.

Standby
Ambulances wait on standby at big public events, ready to the take ill or injured people to the hospital.

Stretcher
Equipment used to move a patient who must stay in a lying position to and from an ambulance.

Index

accident 7, 8, 9, 16, 17
air ambulance 18, 28
airplane ambulance 18, 26, 27
ambulette 25, 28
aspirator 9, 28
attendant 12

baby care clinic 15
battlefield 22, 23
blood 17
breathing machine 9

cabinets 13
communications center 8, 12
crashes 17

defibrillator 9, 28
dressings 17
driver 12
drugs 12

earthquakes 17
emergency ambulance 7, 8, 12, 13, 24
emergency pack 17
equipment 6, 7, 9, 11, 12, 13, 16, 17, 27

fever ambulance 26
fire departments 8, 16
first aid center 24
floods 17
flying ambulance 18
Flying Doctor 26

heart machine 9
helicopter ambulance 6, 7, 10, 11, 18, 21, 22, 23

hospital 6, 9, 14, 17, 18, 21, 22, 24, 25

mobile communications center 16, 28
mountain rescue 14

nurses 17

operating room 13
oxygen 17
oxygen cylinder 13, 28

paramedics 6, 9, 12, 18, 28
police 8, 14, 16
police ambulance 14

radio 10, 16
Red Cross 6, 14, 15, 22, 23, 27
resuscitator 9, 28

signs 10
siren 10
space ambulance 27
splints 17
standby 24, 28
station wagon 14, 15, 25
steam ambulance 27
St. John Ambulance Brigade 24
storage space 13
stretchers 7, 13, 28

transport ambulance 25

war 22
wheelchairs 25

ECONOLINE 350